Guantánamo

Guantánamo
THE BAY OF DISCORD

by Roger Ricardo

Translated by Mary Todd

OCEAN

ISBN paper 1-875284-56-7

First edition, 1994

Printed in Australia

Published by Ocean Press,
GPO Box 3279, Melbourne, Victoria 3001, Australia

Distributed in the USA by The Talman Company,
131 Spring Street, Suite 201E-N, New York, NY 10012, USA
Distributed in Britain and Europe by Central Books,
99 Wallis Road, London E9 5LN, Britain
Distributed in Australia by Astam Books,
57-71 John Street, Leichhardt, NSW 2040, Australia
Distributed in Cuba by Ocean Press,
Apartado 686, C.P. 11300, Havana, Cuba

Contents

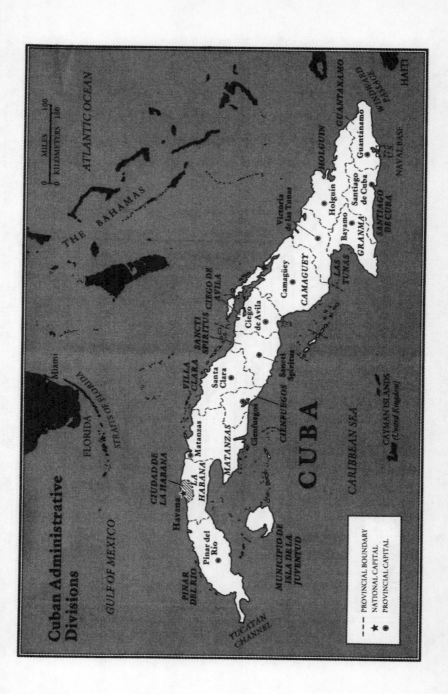

Cuban Administrative Divisions

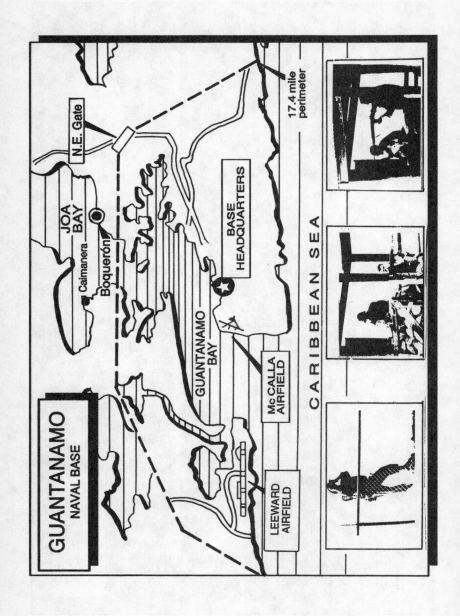

GUANTANAMO
NAVAL BASE

N.E. Gate

JOA BAY

Caimanera

Boquerón

GUANTANAMO BAY

BASE HEADQUARTERS

McCALLA AIRFIELD

LEEWARD AIRFIELD

17.4 mile perimeter

CARIBBEAN SEA

Chapter 1

Symbols and contrasts on the border

Having no official land border with any other country, Cuba, the largest island in the Antilles, is separated by the Caribbean Sea and Atlantic Ocean from its nearest neighbors: Mexico, the United States, the Bahamas, Haiti and Jamaica. Yet Cuba still has a small piece of territory encircled by barbed wire, extensive land mines, and occupied by hostile troops under a foreign flag. This occupied territory is the Guantánamo Naval Base, the United States' oldest overseas military installation. This strip of land in the southeastern corner Cuba is a place of symbols and contrasts.

A sign proclaims "Republic of Cuba. Free territory in the Americas." Facing it, a few steps farther on, is the emblem of the U.S. Marine Corps. The northeast gate provides the only access to the base from unoccupied territory, flanked by a sentry box where Marines keep watch. A few dozen meters away is the sentry box of the Border Patrol of the Cuban Armed Forces.

Every work day, 30 or so Cubans enter the base through that gate in the morning and leave through it at night; they are all who are left of the thousands of Cuban workers once employed on the base. Tension and acts of provocation by the U.S. forces led most of the Cuban workers to leave; others were expelled.

This area wasn't richly endowed by nature, but the landscape is nevertheless quite striking: dozens of watchtowers and observation posts — both Cuban and U.S. — stand as sentinels in the barren land, with kilometer upon kilometer of metal fences dividing "them" from "us". In between, there's a no-man's land. Experts say the U.S. side contains one of the densest mine fields in the world, with an estimated 70,000 antipersonnel and antitank mines. In that seemingly peaceful scene, an animal may set off one of those devices at any moment. Further inside the base, aircraft carriers, battleships, cruisers, destroyers, frigates, submarines, amphibious craft, helicopter carriers and Coast Guard vessels go busily in and out of the immense bay. The bay has 42 anchorages — enough for an entire war fleet.

At the back of the bay, on the Cuban side, are two towns: Caimanera and Boquerón. Theirs was a sad history up until 1959, as U.S. troops from the base used them as enormous brothels — a shameful and offensive situation for the Cuban population which the revolution promptly ended. Now the ports of these towns are used for shipping sugar and for fishing. Cargo ships must reach them via an international channel that passes the gunboats and proving grounds for the planes and artillery of the U.S. Marine Corps. However, the channel is often closed to peaceful shipping — whenever it suits the interests of those who believe themselves the lords and masters of the bay.

The U.S. State Department emphasizes that the main reason for the Guantánamo Naval Base is political. In its view, the greatest power on earth shouldn't have to cede to pressure from a small, poor, communist country. The U.S. Navy adds that Guantánamo is the largest and best base in the world for training purposes, so there is no reason to return it to Cuba.

The weather is nearly always clear and warm in Guantánamo, with an average annual rainfall of 12 inches. The port can accomodate the largest ships in the U.S. Navy; 10 minutes sailing from the mouth of the bay, the water is 100 fathoms deep. There is little sea and air traffic in the area, so maneuvers and artillery exercises can be carried out without concern. The recent increase in these practices on the base has led U.S. families living there to protest against the incessant artillery fire, low-flying planes, constant alarm and troops movements.

It is estimated that over 13,000 acts of provocation by U.S.

troops have been carried out since 1962, demonstrating the anti-Cuban policy of the successive U.S. administrations.

Tool for political blackmail

Secret U.S. government documents that were declassified in early 1992 — foreign policy materials, intelligence assessments and diplomatic information from the 1,191-page *United States Foreign Policy Relations, 1958-1960*, volume VI, "Cuba" — reveal that the United States has been drawing up plans against Cuba for more than three decades, beginning just a month after the January 1959 triumph of the revolution. This document also contains the program of secret actions against Fidel Castro that the special group of the National Security Council's Undercover Activities Commission prepared in late 1960. The way the United States is handling the sensitive question of the Guantánamo Naval Base is instructive.

Researchers and specialists from the United States and other countries suggest the bay has lost its usefulnesss and is, in fact, quite vulnerable. Therefore, the return of the territory wouldn't affect the United States' military plans in any important way. The loss of the enclave's strategic value is evident, for most of the activities and installations have been duplicated, such as at the Roosevelt Roads Naval Station in Puerto Rico. Because of its location, the Guantánamo installation would theoretically play some role in case of a military blockade of Cuba, but its vulnerability suggests that it would not be an essential one.

Even though the base has such geographical advantages as deep water and rapid access to the exercise areas, it is not comparable to the strategic possibilities of other installations in the region. The proximity of Haiti, Jamaica and the Cayman Islands means that maneuvering possibilities in the Guantánamo area are more limited than at the proving grounds in northern Puerto Rico, Antigua and Barbados which face the open Atlantic.

The southeastern approaches to the United States are protected by other U.S. installations in the area, such as Roosevelt Roads; the Panama Canal Zone; Key West; Jacksonville; and the Hydroacoustic Detection Center, in the Bahamas. In addition, McDill and Homestead Air Force Bases in Florida maintain air and naval patrols. Battle groups headed by aircraft carriers or destroyers protect the area's ports, demonstrating the Navy's ability to redistribute its forces among its bases on the mainland and offer more dynamic and modern naval coverage for the main points of its coast.

It is clear that the Guantánamo Naval Base is, above all, a symbol of U.S. power, with the United States controlling a portion of Cuba's territory against the will of its people. At the same time, the possibility of the base serving as a tool for blackmail — to obtain future concessions from Cuba — should not be ruled out. During the October 1962 Missile Crisis sources close to the White House stated that Adlai Stevenson, then U.S. ambassador to the United Nations, had suggested to President Kennedy that he include Guantánamo in a possible project for reaching an agreement with the Soviet Union. But apparently the president had replied that the timing wasn't right. This indicates two things: the insignificant military value Guantánamo had at that time and its increasing role as a political tool.

It is important to note that Cuban President Fidel Castro stated during that crisis that the withdrawal of the U.S. troops from the Guantánamo Naval Base and the return of the territory to its legitimate owners would provide Cuba with a guarantee that the United States would not eliminate the island. For Cuba, the presence of U.S. troops in that enclave constitutes both a threat to international peace and security and a threat to its national security.

In diverse international forums, Cuba has called for respect for its rights and has been supported by the international community. For example, the Movement of Nonaligned Countries stated in its First Summit Conference, held in Belgrade in 1961, that "the North American military base at Guantánamo, Cuba, the presence of which has been opposed by the government and people of Cuba, affects the sovereignty and territorial integrity of that country." In later meetings, that Third World organization ratified its support for Cuba's demand. Within that context, some U.S. political experts consider that the Guantánamo base should be returned because, since Cuba is a nonaligned country, it would be obliged not to turn any of its territory over to another foreign country for use as a military base.

It should be noted that Cuba's call for the return of the area that the United States occupies illegally is based on the principle of sovereignty and implies opposition to any other similar situation. Cuba never had any intention of establishing a base there or of turning Guantánamo over to another foreign power if the United States had returned it — not even when the Soviet Union was cooperating militarily with Cuba. Cuba's agreements with the Soviet Union were always in accord with Cuba's foreign policy, which was based on the principles of independence and the defense of Cuban sovereignty.

An unwelcome neighbor

With binoculars, you can see Cuba's unwelcome neighbor from El Picote Hill, in the eastern sector of the Cuban border. The Guantánamo Naval Base covers an area of nearly 118 square kilometers, 49.4 of which are solid ground; 38.8, water; and 29.4, swampland. Around 7,000 people are stationed within the compound permanently; more than 3,000 are military personnel, and the rest, their families and support personnel. In addition, there is a floating population of thousands, such as crews in transit, the exact figure depending on the number and kind of ships in port.

The residents live in the Villamar, Bargo, Deer Point, Villamar Extension and other neighborhoods, depending on their social class and position in the military hierarchy. Sherman Avenue leads from the residential area to the port installations and other key areas of the base. Every month, several dozen ships of the U.S. Atlantic Fleet and planes of various kinds enter and leave the base on supply, instruction and anti-drug trafficking missions, according to U.S. authorities, although they also use this cover to keep a group that is ready to participate in any kind of military action in the Caribbean area. The U.S. troops also engage in reconnaissance missions against Cuba.

The United States has two airfields in the base: McCalla, to the east, and Tres Piedras, also called Leeward Point — the larger and more active of the two — to the west. The proving ground for planes and target area for the artillery — 155-mm howitzers emplaced at Cable Beach, to the east, and on Toro Norte and Toro Sur Cays — is also to the west, in the swampy San Nicolás area near the bay. Important military sites, such as command and observation posts and radar positions, are on the eastern heights.

The base has a hospital, warehouses, powder magazines, obstacle courses and shooting ranges for infantry and tanks, as well as quarters for the troops (such as Bulkeley). It also has a desalination plant that can process more than a million gallons of water a day. However, occasionally water has had to be brought from the United States. The desalination plant was built very quickly when the Cuban government cut off supplies of drinking water to the base on February 6, 1964, after the U.S. authorities had kidnapped and imprisoned 38 Cuban fishermen, and armed pirate vessels based in Florida had repeatedly attacked Cuban fishing boats.

Estimates in several U.S. publications state that over $100 million has been spent on the base's installations. Even so, a budget of around $35 million was approved in 1992 to modernize and enlarge them — a sure sign of the U.S. authorities' determination not to abandon this Cuban territory. Thus, the U.S. government is spending millions on Guantánamo — for which, under the lease signed in February 1903, it is supposed to pay 2,000 gold coins a year for as long as it occupies the base (an amount now worth $4,085 a year). This means that for this huge area, the United States owes Cuba anuual rent of less than a cent per square meter of land.

However, since the triumph of the revolution, the Cuban authorities has not cashed a single check from the U.S. government for rent for the base, convinced that no money on earth could purchase Cuba's sovereignty over that illegally occupied territory. Those checks and the $14,000 a month that the United States used to pay for water supplied to the base were the only two financial links the United States maintained with Cuba when, more than 30 years ago, it imposed the harshest and longest economic blockade that one country has ever imposed against another in times of "peace."

These are the symbols and contrasts on the border, where only a few centimeters from the area occupied by the United

States stands a royal palm, Cuba's national tree, straight and tall on the semi-desert plain asserting that this land is Cuban.

Chapter 2

An old dream, a long nightmare

A few weeks after his inauguration as president, Thomas Jefferson called his closest friends together to swap ideas about the future of the young, impetuous United States. In that meeting, Jefferson clearly defined one key aspect of his foreign policy when he said he had always viewed Cuba as the most interesting addition that could be made to the nation. The United States had for a long time cast covetous eyes on Cuba. Its expansionist intentions were manifest very soon after it obtained its own independence from England, when the Caribbean island was still a Spanish colony.

John Adams, second president of the United States, was the first U.S. government leader to express what was to be the United States' attitude toward Cuba in the late 18th and all of the 19th century: Cuba should remain in Spanish hands until the time came when it could be seized by the United States. Above all, it should never be independent. In a letter to Robert R. Livingston, Adams wrote on June 23, 1783, that the Caribbean island was a natural extension of the American continent, and, therefore, it was impossible to resist the conviction that the annexation of Cuba to the Federal Republic was indispensable for the continuation of the Union.

In 1823, the U.S. government outlined the two concepts that were to determine the relations between that nation and the neighboring Caribbean island: the doctrine of the Manifest

Destiny and the theory of the ripe fruit. Both are based on the use of military might as a tool of foreign policy and the U.S. determination to impose its way of life as the highest form of civilization — precepts which are apparently still pillars of U.S. foreign relations.

John Quincy Adams, secretary of state in the Monroe administration and Monroe's successor as president, gave those concepts their most original formulation, employing the law of gravity from physics in his ripe fruit theory in the sphere of politics:

> ... if an apple, severed by the tempest from its native tree, cannot but fall to the ground, Cuba, forcibly disjoined from its unnatural connection with Spain and incapable of self-support, can gravitate only to the North American Union, which, by the same law of nature, cannot cast her off from its bosom.

Knocking the fruit down

Seven and a half decades after John Quincy Adams' prediction, the United States declared war on a battered and exhausted Spain — just when the Cuban patriots' independence army was about to achieve victory after 30 years of intermittent armed struggle against the Spanish crown. On April 11, 1898, President McKinley sent the U.S. Congress his long-awaited message on the United States' relations with Spain and the war in Cuba, requesting authorization to intervene in the conflict. The House of Representatives and Senate debated the issue for several days; on April 19, they issued their Joint Resolution. The next day, McKinley signed it into law, turning it into an ultimatum that triggered war with Spain.

The United States never recognized the Cuban people's struggle for independence, their Governments in Arms or their status as a legitimate party to the conflict. A few hours after declaring war on Spain, the U.S. president said it wouldn't be wise for the United States to recognize the independence of the so-called Republic of Cuba at that time because, if it were to do so and intervene, its conduct would be subject to the approval or disapproval of such a government; then it would have to either submit to its leadership or enter into a friendly alliance with it.

All this shows that the United States' interest in "liberating" Cuba was simply an expression of its determination to keep the island from becoming independent, sweep Spain out of the Caribbean and seize that area of influence for itself. The blowing up of the *Maine* in Havana Bay was engineered as a pretext for the United States to intervene in the war. The battleship, which had arrived in Cuba on a "courtesy visit," was blown up on February 15, 1898, and the war ended with U.S. military occupation of the island.

The U.S. press at the time mounted an enormous campaign supporting the government's action. One newspaper, for example, carried a photograph showing what it claimed was the hole made in the *Maine* by a Spanish torpedo. Later, it turned out that the photo had been published the previous year — and was of an eclipse of the sun. Over 80 years had to pass before the U.S. authorities acknowledged that the Spanish hadn't blown up the *Maine*. Then, U.S. specialists admitted that the explosion had taken place on board, in a tiny ammunition store in the prow, as stated in Admiral G.H. Rickover's book *How the Maine was destroyed*.

Extermination memo

The U.S. government's political pragmatism toward Cuba was expressed in its complete lack of respect for the Cuban people, as evident in a memo by Under-Secretary of War J.C. Breckenridge. Writing from Washington on December 24, 1897, to Lieutenant General N.S. Miles of the U.S. Army, who had been named general-in-chief of the intervention forces, Breckenridge instructed him how to carry out the war. He said that Cuba was larger and had a greater population than Puerto Rico and that its population consisted of whites, blacks, Asians and mestizos — who, in Breckenridge's opinion, were generally indolent and apathetic. He said that, naturally, the immediate annexation of those elements to the U.S. federation would be madness, and, before suggesting any such thing, the U.S. forces should cleanse Cuba — if necessary, by employing the same means which Divine

Providence applied to Sodom and Gomorrah.

Specifically, Breckenridge argued that the United States would have to destroy everything within range of its cannon and mercilessly tighten the blockade so that hunger and pestilence, its constant companion, would decimate Cuba's peaceful population and reduce its army. The allied army should be employed constantly in scouting forays; be always in the vanguard so that, caught between two fires, it would bear the brunt of the war; and be assigned all of the dangerous and hopeless expeditions. Summing up, the note said that U.S. policy should consist of always supporting the weaker against the stronger until the extermination of both Cubans and Spaniards had been attained and the United States could annex the Pearl of the Antilles. He could hardly have been more explicit.

In their efforts to prevent Cuba's independence, the U.S. authorities also had the support of certain economic circles on the island, such as the sugar magnates, who had commercial ties with their powerful neighbor. Both the owners of the Cuban sugar industry — the country's main source of income — and the government officials in Washington knew that the Cuban people bitterly opposed annexation and were ready to continue fighting rather than see another form of domination imposed. That factor was largely responsible for the U.S. authorities changing their annexationist plan and apparent acceptance of the Cuban people's desire for independence.

The Cuban response

General Máximo Gómez, one of the fathers of Cuban independence who became Commander-in-Chief of the Mambí Liberation Army, clearly expressed the Cuban people's thinking on the U.S. military intervention. On January 8, 1899, he wrote in his campaign diary as follows:

> The Americans' military occupation of the country is too high a price to pay for their spontaneous intervention in the war we waged against Spain for freedom and independence. The American government's attitude toward the heroic Cuban people at this history-making time is, in my opinion,

one of big business. This situation is dangerous for the country, mortifying the public spirit and hindering organization in all of the branches that, from the outset, should provide solid foundations for the future republic, when everything was entirely the work of all the inhabitants of the island, without distinction of nationality.

Nothing is more rational and fair than that the owner of the house should be the to live in it with his family and be the one who furnishes and decorates it as he likes and that he not be forced against his will and inclination to follow norms imposed by his neighbor.

All these considerations lead me to think that Cuba cannot have true moral peace — which is what the people need for their happiness and good fortune — under the transitional government. This transitional government was imposed by force by a foreign power and, therefore, is illegitimate and incompatible with the principles that the entire country has been upholding for so long and in the defense of which half of its sons have given their lives and all of its wealth has been consumed.

There is so much natural anger and grief throughout the island that the people haven't really been able to celebrate the triumph of the end of their former rulers' power.

They have left in sadness, and in sadness we have remained, because a foreign power has replaced them. I dreamed of peace with Spain; I hoped to bid farewell with respect to the brave Spanish soldiers with whom we always met, face to face, on the field of battle. The words *peace* and *freedom* should inspire only love and fraternity on the morning of concord between those who were combatants the night before; but, with their guardianship imposed by force, the Americans have turned the Cubans' victorious joy to bitterness and haven't sweetened the grief of the vanquished.

The situation that has been created for this people — one of material poverty and of grief because their sovereignty has been curbed — is ever more distressing. It is possible that, by the time this strange situation finally ends, the Americans will have snuffed out even the last spark of goodwill.

The first bite

Within the space of eight months, Cuba saw U.S. military intervention; the defeat of the Spanish crown; an end to the fighting; and a series of hostile actions taken by the interventionist forces against the Cuban independence fighters, who were those who had really won the war.

The naval battle of Santiago de Cuba and the seizure of that city in southeastern Cuba were decisive acts in the course of the war and accelerated the peace negotiations. The Treaty of Paris, which ended the war, was signed on December 10, 1898. The U.S. authorities, who acted as if Cuba were a conquered country, negotiated with the Spanish colonial rulers, and both excluded the Cuban people's representatives from the peace talks. Tied hand and foot, Cuba was turned over to the United States.

President McKinley set forth the United States' real intentions concerning Cuba in his December 5, 1899, message to Congress, in which he said that Cuba had, of necessity, to be attached to his nation by special organic or conventional ties — fancy words for annexation and a formula that would guarantee it.

It didn't take long for the president's wishes to be carried out. On March 2, 1901, while considering a military appropriations bill, the U.S. Congress added an amendment authorizing the U.S. president to leave the government and rule of the island of Cuba in the hands of the Cuban people. But this would only happen after a government had been established on the island under a constitution in which, either as an integral part or as an attached statute, the future relations of the United States with Cuba were to be outlined.

This became known as the Platt Amendment because it was presented by Senator Orville Platt, although it had been drafted by Elihu Root. Thus, the first bite was taken of what John Quincy Adams had called the "ripe fruit."

Under this amendment attached to the constitution, the United States limited Cuban sovereignty and turned it into a neocolony; it retroactively legalized U.S. military intervention in the island; it assumed the right to seize a part of Cuba's national territory by leaving the ownership of the Isle of Pines (the second

largest island in the Cuban archipelago, south of the Cuban
mainland) to be adjusted by future treaty; it limited Cuba's rights
to enter into treaties, contract debts and even set up sanitation
programs; and, most opprobious of all, forced the country to sell
or lease a part of its territory for the establishment of naval
stations.

With the July 1903 Permanent Treaty, a piece of Cuban
territory was handed over to the United States — for which Cuba
was to receive 2,000 gold coins a year for as long as the United
States should wish to occupy and use that area. Thus, the U.S.
Guantánamo Naval Base was born.

Guantánamo Bay

When Christopher Columbus sailed into Guantánamo Bay on
April 30, 1494, during his second voyage to the New World, he
named it Great Port, describing it in his diary as "a broad bay
with dark water, of unsuspected dimensions." In 1500, however,
when his cartographer made a map of the lands that had been
discovered, he called it Guantánamo, because that's what the
Cuban Indians living near the bay called their region. The Indians
themselves had called the bay Joa, after a cactus with a red fruit
similar to a tomato that abounded in its vicinity.

No use was made of the magnificent port until 1741, when a
squadron of the English fleet arrived and, under the command of
the Admiral Edward Vernon, tried (in vain) to conquer the
eastern part of Cuba from there. The men of the fleet left some
fortifications on what, ever since, has been known as Loma de los
Ingleses (Englishmen's Hill) and the beginning of a settlement
which they called Cumberland — where, many years later, the
present town of Caimanera was built.

The first contact the United States had with the bay was in
June 1898, when Admiral Simpson seized it and landed around
600 Marines during the Spanish-Cuban-American War. On that
occasion, the Spanish troops stationed in the area attacked the
Marines soon after their landing and would have defeated them if
it hadn't been for the Cuban Liberation Army, which entered the
battle and kept the U.S. forces from being crushed.

Paradoxically, the U.S. forces' use of Guantánamo Bay was

decided nearby, in Santiago de Cuba, after the fighting that led to the culmination of what Secretary of State John Hay, in a letter to President Theodore Roosevelt, was to call "the splendid little war."

An absolutely necessary strategic base

On March 24, 1902, Tomás Estrada Palma, president of Cuba, and Theodore Roosevelt, president of the United States, met in the White House. Roosevelt told Estrada Palma which places had been chosen for establishing naval or coaling stations, as stipulated in clause VII of the Platt Amendment: Cienfuegos and Guantánamo, on the southern coast, and Nipe and Honda Bays, on the northern coast. Later, in the Permanent Treaty of 1903, reference was made only to the leasing of Guantánamo and Honda Bays.

On December 12, 1903, control of the Cuban territory on Guantánamo Bay that was to be leased was officially handed over to the United States in a ceremony held on board the battleship *Kearsage*, flagship of the squadron of the Atlantic Fleet. In accord with the note the Cuban government had sent to the United States, requesting that the ceremony be kept low key because the Cuban people were protesting against the lease, only one Cuban was present. At noon on that day, the Cuban flag was lowered while a 21-gun salute was fired, and the U.S. flag was raised in its stead. That was all. Soon after, around 600 U.S. troops landed.

Thus, the United States took possession of a key point in the Caribbean Sea, ensuring its military control of the area, control over the Panama Canal and the rapid deployment of its forces to any point in Central or South America. Theodore Roosevelt recognized the importance of Guantánamo when, in a message to Congress, he described it as the "absolutely necessary strategic base" for controlling the Caribbean and the route to the Panama Canal.

Not content with what it had obtained, in 1912 the United States imposed another agreement for extending the boundaries of Guantánamo in exchange for giving up Honda Bay — which, obviously, had little importance to its strategic plans. With that expansion, the United States could control nearly all the bay —

especially its access channel, which, it had been agreed at first would be shared so as to guarantee free trade by the Cuban ports of Caimanera and Boquerón. This too was conceded under threat of intervention.

"Good neighbor..."

The U.S. authorities used the Guantánamo base for their subsequent invasions of the Dominican Republic, Haiti, Nicaragua, Mexico and Panama — demonstrating the "Big Stick" policy in the first two decades of this century.

In response to the Cuban's people unwavering opposition to the actions of the U.S. authorities; the Cuban revolutionary process of 1933; and the economic crisis that scourged the United States at the time, President Franklin D. Roosevelt proposed the "Good Neighbor Policy." The application of this concept in U.S. foreign policy toward the rest of the hemisphere had repercussions in Cuba with the 1934 signing of the Treaty of Reciprocity. While that document repealed the Platt Amendment and the Permanent Treaty of 1903, it maintained all the stipulations concerning the leasing of the Guantánamo base — that is, it left the running sore of Cuban-U.S. relations to fester.

Moreover, at the same time the document establishing the United States' "Good Neighbor" policy toward Cuba was being signed in Washington, over 20 U.S. warships of the Atlantic Fleet made a "friendly visit" to the Bay of Havana and other points along the island's coasts.

The dagger of words and deeds

Some say that words on paper are one thing, and their application, another. The same could well be said of the history of U.S. policy toward Cuba, in which the Guantánamo Naval Base is an excellent example. The Joint Resolution of the House and Senate of the United States declared that the Cuban people were and by right ought to be free and independent and that the United States had no intention or desire of exercising sovereignty, jurisdiction or rule in Cuba except for the purpose of pacifying the island.

In the Treaty of Paris, the U.S. government stated that, as

long as its occupation of the island of Cuba should last, it would assume and fulfill the obligations under international law to protect life and property. The Paris meeting was followed by the July 25, 1900, Constitutional Convention in Cuba, which was to implement the Joint Resolution by drafting the Constitution and agree to the stipulations concerning the bilateral relations between the United States and Cuba.

The Platt Amendment was attached to a military appropriations bill in the United States on March 2, 1901 — many months after the Cuban Constitutional Convention had been called, its members had been empowered to draft the Cuban Constitution and they had concluded their deliberations.

At that time, Enrique Villuendas, one of the members of the Constitutional Convention, stated: "The amendment demands of the members of the Convention that we accept conditions, but, when the Cuban people voted to confer on us the mandate contained in the call for the Convention, they asked only for wording and style." Thus, as an appendix to the Constitution, the Platt Amendment is unconstitutional — and, therefore, everything emanating from it cannot be legally binding.

Coercion and fraud were constants in the process leading to the establishment of the U.S. military enclave in Cuba — factors that, under international law, make any agreement null and void. The following example is very eloquent. In a letter to Secretary Root, General Leonard Wood, U.S. military governor of Cuba, wrote that the time had come to establish the position of the government with absolute clarity and that it should be done in the form of an ultimatum, so that all discussion would cease.

General Wood also warned the Cuban Convention that it shouldn't modify the Amendment and that the U.S. troops wouldn't leave Cuba until the terms of the Amendment had been adopted. So there should be no possible misunderstanding, his warning wound up by saying that, if the Amendment weren't accepted, there would be no Republic. Clearly, consent was obtained under duress.

Sovereignty and the law

International law establishes the principle of consent as the basis for any legal obligation resulting from an agreement on the establishment of those ties. Therefore, the agreements on the Guantánamo base should be annulled by reason of lack of consent, since that precept was not observed. Likewise, consent is determined by the aim and cause. The question arises of what became of the cause of maintaining Cuba's independence — which was put forward at the beginning of the century — and of what, in the light of facts past and present, happened with the friendship between the two countries.

A further example of the violation of international legal norms are the terms of the lease of the bay. The agreements ignore the temporary nature of any lease and expresses an intention to lease it in perpetuity. In fact, it is absurd to think that the owner of anything that is leased cannot recover it at a given time, because any lease is, per se, temporary.

Moreover, international law consecrates the precept of basic changes of circumstance, which means that, when the circumstances which gave rise to an agreement change, the agreement may be considered ineffective, inapplicable or null and void. It is obvious that, after the triumph of the revolution in 1959, the base became a tool of aggression, not friendship.

Therefore, the base should have been returned to Cuba in January 1961, when the United States broke off diplomatic relations with the island. At the time, however, the Eisenhower administration stated unilaterally that the United States would retain the base, abrogating to itself the right of decision that pertained to the government with which it was breaking its ties.

An act of force

At the beginning of the century, the Guantánamo Naval Base was of strategic importance in the United States' military policy, and that importance was the reason for its creation. Now, this is no longer the case. Nor does the pretext of the East-West confrontation any longer exist. Therefore, the Cuban government regards the United States' retention of the base as an unmitigated act of force and a permanent offense to Cuba's national dignity and sovereignty.

Under Cuban Constitutional law, sovereignty pertains to the

nation, and no ruler is empowered to sign or ratify pacts or treaties that limit or impair national sovereignty or the nation's territorial integrity in any way. At the time the land for the base was leased, the Cuban government was not in fact empowered to cede any part of the country in perpetuity. Moreover, the present Constitution of the Republic of Cuba — which was approved by 97.7 percent of the voters in a referendum held on February 24, 1976 — states (chapter 1, paragraph 10) that the Cuban nation repudiates and considers illegal and null and void all treaties, pacts or concessions that are arrived at in conditions of inequality or that relinquish or diminish its sovereignty over any portion of its national territory.

Chapter 3

Flesh and blood

At the age of 19 and as a soldier in the defense of his homeland, Ramón López Peña had hopes of eventually becoming an agricultural machinery mechanic. He probably would have done just that if two U.S. sentries at the Guantánamo Naval Base hadn't shot him dead. It was after 7 p.m. on July 19, 1964. The provocations from the U.S. sentry box had escalated from shouted insults to obscene gestures and stone throwing. The Cubans sentries remained calm, not responding to any of the hostile acts, but suddenly two Marines in the U.S. sentry box threw themselves on the floor and with automatic rifles shot at the Cuban sentry box some meters away.

Ramón was standing guard at the time and was ordered to seek protection in the trench along with his comrades, but another burst of fire mowed him down before he got there. Mortally wounded, he died 20 minutes later. However, Ramón was by no means the first Cuban to be murdered by the U.S. Marines in and from that occupied territory. The history of acts of aggression and provocation centering around the Guantánamo Naval Base began as soon as the base was established. Prior to the revolution in January 1959, such actions were the main expression of the United States' utter scorn for Cuban rights and lack of respect for Cuba's national integrity. After 1959, the Guantánamo base became a constant source of friction aimed at providing a pretext for possible U.S. armed intervention in Cuba.

Cuba, the base's backyard

After its 19th-century intervention in Cuba, the United States considered everything to do with the island to be part of its domestic policy. Thus Cuban patriot Juan Gualberto Gómez's words to the Constitutional Convention at the beginning of this century were prophetic: "The [Platt] Amendment was like giving it the key to our house so it could come and go at all hours." And that was just what the United States did until 1959. Cuba was seen as nothing more than the backyard of the Guantánamo Naval Base.

In 1912, supported by the Platt Amendment, the troops stationed at the base occupied various parts of the eastern region of the country to crush an armed uprising against the Cuban government — even though the government had not asked them for help. Some years later, in that same part of the island, U.S. troops occupied the railroads when the railway workers called a strike against the U.S.-owned rail company.

On December 17, 1940, a U.S. foreman in charge of work at the base murdered Lino Rodríguez, a Cuban construction worker. Fishermen from Caimanera found his body in the bay with marks of a brutal beating and bullet wounds. The foreman later confessed to the attack but was never duly punished by the U.S. authorities.

In September 1954, a Cuban worker Lorenzo Salomón was arrested and then tortured for 15 days. The U.S. authorities said he had embezzled money, but they never presented any evidence to the Cuban authorities — who were the only ones empowered to take any action. The Cuban government in that period usually displayed a thoroughly servile tolerance of whatever abuses were committed by U.S. personnel. The same tolerance was shown toward the rampages of U.S. Marines and sailors through the Cuban towns, such as Caimanera, the town nearest the base.

Caimanera, with a population of about 8,000 at that time, became a center of prostitution, gambling and drugs serving the U.S. troops. It had over 60 brothels, with around 700 prostitutes. Signs such as "Arizona Bar" and "Marilyn Bar" flanked its long main street. These places were for the enlisted men, while the officers had a more elegant club fronting the town's main square.

The U.S. troops engaged in fights, abuses of all kinds, acts of public aggression and disrespect for the Cuban authorities, who were powerless to establish order, because the Cuban laws weren't applicable to the Marines and sailors even when they were in Cuban territory.

During the struggle against the regime of General Batista (1952-58) — a de facto government that had first the complicity and then the recognition and support of the United States — the base served as a center supplying fuel and ammunition to the dictatorship's planes that indiscriminately bombed rural areas and defenseless towns. Photographs taken on the base landing strips while the planes took on those supplies were published in the U.S. press and in newspapers in other parts of the world as irrefutable proof of the support the United States was giving to the Batista regime while the revolutionary forces were fighting in the mountains in the eastern part of the country.

Escalation of incidents

The triumph of the Cuban revolution meant an end to the status quo for the United States' geopolitical aspirations in Latin America and the Caribbean. Cuba proved to be an irritating pebble in the shoe of U.S. interests, and U.S. ruling circles immediately unleashed their hostility against the island. The Guantánamo Naval Base became a permanent focal point of conflicts.

On January 12, 1961 — just a few days after the United States broke off diplomatic relations with Cuba — Manuel Prieto González, a worker at the base, was arrested, accused of being an agent of the Cuban revolutionary government. He was tortured and forced to swallow pills containing poison. Two months later, early on the morning of March 13, 1961, a pirate boat coming from the base shot at the Santiago de Cuba oil refinery with heavy-caliber machine guns and 57-mm cannon. Cuban sailor René Rodríguez was killed in that attack, which also seriously damaged the plant.

On September 30 of that same year, Rubén López Sabariego, a worker at the base, was arrested by the Military Intelligence Service. Eighteen days later, a U.S. official notified López

Sabariego's wife that his body had been found in a ditch on the base. Medical examination of his body showed that he had been beaten to death. Former Lieutenant William A. Szili of the U.S. Navy, one of the accessories to the crime, told a *Philadelphia Bulletin* reporter that Captain Arthur J. Jackson had finished the Cuban worker off with some shots.

Rodolfo Rosell Salas, a fisherman, was kidnapped, tortured and savagely murdered in the U.S. military enclave in May 1962. His mutilated body, bearing stab wounds, was found in his boat, adrift in the bay near Caimanera. On August 23, 1963, the U.S. destroyer *DD 864* ran down the Cuban schooner *Joven Amalia* at the entrance to Guantánamo Bay. Cuban photographer Berto Belén was wounded in the right hand and ear on February 23, 1965, shot while he was preparing to take pictures of an act of provocation and holding his camera at eye level — which showed that the shot was intended to kill.

On numerous occasions U.S. Marines have also shot at the Cuban flag near the northeast gate. In contrast, the Cuban sentries show respect when the U.S. flag is raised or lowered in the same area. U.S. Marines shooting at Cuban sentry boxes killed Ramón López Peña in 1964 and Luis Ramírez López in 1966, both members of the Border Patrol. In other acts of aggression against Cuban sentry boxes, they wounded soldiers Luis Ramírez Reyes, Antonio Campos and Andrés Noel Larduet.

After López Peña's death, the Cuban government took a series of measures to prevent incidents at the border so the U.S. authorities couldn't claim that Cuba was the aggressor. Among other things, the Cuban sentry boxes were moved back from the dividing line and fortifications built and a security strip was completed in 1970. This was an important step that required considerable human and material resources. Far from responding positively to Cuba's efforts in this regard, the United States launched a new phase of aggression.

Center of counterrevolutionary operations
The base also became a reception center for those who, charged with murder and torture, were fleeing from Cuban justice. The U.S. authorities gave asylum to nearly 1,000 known murderers

and henchmen of Batista's dictatorship. Some of them were later sent out to infiltrate Cuban territory, carrying out acts of sabotage and organizing armed groups in the nearby mountain areas after U.S. military personnel had given them training on the base.

Between 1959 and 1962, before an effective system of vigilance and defense had been established on the border, the U.S. military enclave was an important center of counterrevolutionary operations that the CIA directed through the Naval Intelligence Service. Liaison agents with the counterrevolutionary organizations that operated in some parts of Cuban territory were sent out from the base; in particular, weapons and other matériel for insurrectional groups and means for sabotaging the economy were sent into the eastern part of the country, and plans were hatched for assassinating leaders of the revolution.

A revealing example of such deeds was the plan drawn up on the base for mounting an "attack" against itself as a pretext for the United States to intervene militarily in Cuba — a plan that Ernesto Che Guevara denounced in the Inter-American Economic and Social Council meeting that was held in Punta del Este, Uruguay, in 1961. That plan, called "Immediate Action," which was exposed by individuals who were in contact with the military chief of the base, included an assassination attempt against Raúl Castro during the mass meeting held in Santiago de Cuba, near the base, to celebrate July 26.

"Immediate Action" called for placing no less than four mortars on a farm adjoining the naval base. They were to fire six shells against the U.S. enclave. At the same time, another mortar was to start firing against a nearby artillery emplacement of the Cuban Army, so that, believing itself under attack from the base, it would start shooting. Thus, a pretext would be created for U.S. military intervention in Cuba. Captain Caels E. Echemnweiss, who was chief of the base at the time, was one of the most active promoters of the plot, but his view of the plan of action, along with the final decision-making, were in contradiction with the CIA project. Subsequent commentaries suggested that this friction led to Captain Echemnweiss being replaced by Rear Admiral Edward J. O'Donnell as commander of the naval base.

Cuban intelligence uncovered the conspiracy. The plotters

Guantánamo Bay looking inland from the sea. The upper bay is controlled by Cuba.

Funeral for Luis Ramírez López

Rodolfo Rosell

Luis Ramírez López

Ramón López Peña

Cuban guard post after being fired upon from U.S. side on December 7, 1989

The Northeast Gate at Guantánamo base. The only route between the Cuban side and the occupied territory of the U.S. base.

U.S. soldier at Guantánamo base

U.S. soldiers initiating provocations against Cuban guard posts, including aiming with rifles

Puerta Terrestre at Guantánamo base. Upper part shows U.S. military post while in foreground is a Cuban post.

U.S. guard post at edge of military base in Guantánamo

were arrested, including José Amparo Rosabal, one of the main ringleaders, who had sought refuge in the Guantánamo base after the mercenary invasion at the Bay of Pigs in 1961. When asked about the weapons which were taken from them, Rosabal and his accomplices stated that U.S. troops on the base had given them weapons, which they took into Cuban territory at a point on the border three miles from Boquerón — the same place where, years later, Luis Ramírez López was murdered.

Since 1960, as part of a plan to ease the pressure that militiamen and members of the Rebel Army were exerting against the groups of counterrevolutionaries who had taken up arms in the Escambray — a mountainous area in the middle of the country — the CIA used the base to link similar armed bands in the mountains near Guantánamo and Baracoa. A total of five counterrevolutionary groups were organized from the base, but they didn't survive their first armed actions. Those who weren't captured sought refuge in the U.S. military enclave.

The Cuban authorities have also uncovered several conspiracies organized by agents recruited on the base. When Ricardo Fernández Blanco, one of the ringleaders, was arrested, he confessed that he had ties with a Major Morrison of Naval Intelligence. Another captured agent Cornelio Lewis Philips, a Jamaican employed on the base, said he had been given a CIA course on how to obtain military and economic information and to provide support for the counterrevolutionary bands in the area. He stated that he reported directly to the admiral in charge of the U.S. military base.

Inside or out

The many hostile acts the U.S. government carried out on the base have also included actions against the Cubans employed in the enclave — including their wholesale firing as a political reprisal. The U.S. military installation had employed thousands of Cubans. When it was fortified and enlarged during World War II, nearly 10,000 Cubans worked on the base. Later, that number dropped to around 6,000. Some of these workers were seasonal workers, while others were permanent.

After the revolution, political tensions and the breaking of diplomatic relations between Cuba and the United States further reduced the Cuban workforce. At the time of the October 1962 Missile Crisis, around 3,500 Cubans still worked at the base, but between February and May 1964 the U.S. government laid off more than 700 Cuban employees, most of them with more than 20 years' service and unblemished records — as attested to by certificates and diplomas issued by the U.S. authorities themselves.

The workers were given a simple ultimatum: stay on the base and renounce your Cuban citizenship, or go home right now. Choose: inside or out. The U.S. authorities made efforts to persuade some of them, saying that Fidel Castro's government wouldn't stay in power more than a few days. In many cases, the employee was approached at work, told to choose immediately or be put in a vehicle and deposited at the northeast gate.

Six percent of the wages of all those Cuban men and women had been withheld to form a retirement fund — as part of their contracts — but those who opted to leave were never able to draw on it. All are entitled to claim pensions from the U.S. government — a sum that, all told, amounted to over $4 million by the end of 1991.

One of the former base employees, Emilio Samson, was informed by the Office of Personnel Management in Washington, D.C., 25 years after he was thrown off the base, that he had accumulated a little over $36,000. Another, Waldo Limonta, was informed that his pension had been increased by $68 a month from January 1, 1981, and then amounted to $780 a month. None of those workers has been able to collect a cent, however, because the economic blockade that the United States has maintained against Cuba for more than 30 years deprives them of access to their funds. The U.S. reply is always the same: it won't give money to "Castro's communist government."

The former Guantánamo workers even presented their case to Javier Pérez de Cuéllar, then Secretary-General of the United Nations, and he referred the matter to the UN Human Rights Commission. They also presented it to U.S. Congressman Michael Bilivak, the commander of the base and the Vatican (through the Papal Nuncio in Havana), with no success to date.

The overwhelming majority of those men and women are now over 60 years old; some have died. The only support they have received came from the government of Cuba, which granted them protection under the social security laws in effect in the country and found jobs for them as soon as they were fired by the U.S. authorities.

Daily acts of provocation

From 1962 through April 1992, the U.S. base personnel carried out 13,255 acts of provocation from the occupied territory — an average of 441.8 a year, 36.8 a month, or 1.2 a day. The most common forms of aggression against the Cuban sentry boxes have been offensive language, obscene gestures, or pornographic acts; the throwing of stones and other objects; violations of the dividing line and of Cuba's airspace and territorial waters; rifle and pellet gunshots; and aiming such weapons, cannon, tanks and machine guns toward the unoccupied territory.

The acts of provocations have included breaking the fence around the base, climbing the fence, using fire hoses to douse the Cuban side of the line, landing military helicopters in the unoccupied area and using reflectors to illuminate the Cuban sentry boxes. The Cuban government has sent notes to the U.S. government protesting all these acts of provocation and aggression, but, in the vast majority of the cases, it has received no reply in accord with international law.

The international community has been made aware of these constant provocations and of the evidence Cuba has presented to support its protests in many forums, especially the United Nations and the Movement of Nonaligned Countries. Foreign correspondents accredited in Cuba and special envoys from the most diverse media outlets, including those of the United States, have visited the border guarded by the Cuban troops to learn of the violations on the spot and to speak with witnesses.

Cuba has presented evidence of these acts of aggression for more than 30 years and none of the U.S. administrations has been able to deny the charges, for they are irrefutable. At the same time, no-one has ever been able to present any proof of violations of the occupied territory of Guantánamo by Cuban border guards.

Will he be the last?

1966

Luis Ramírez López was the last person shot down by U.S. sentries while standing guard at the border with the occupied area. His case was the only one which the U.S. authorities, through their State Department, have acknowledged and, in an attempt to justify the crime, clearly resorted to lies. The U.S. government stated that the Cuban soldier had entered the territory of the base and that a Marine first fired a warning shot to get him to stop and then, when he kept on coming, fired again, killing him.

If Ramírez López had attempted the action attributed to him by the U.S. authorities, he would have had to climb over three fences, each two meters high and topped with a piece of galvanized metal in the form of an "X" with three strands of barbed wire on each of its top pieces, or cut through the heavy wire mesh of those fences with special wire cutters in daylight, in full view of the well-armed Marines who keep close watch on the base's perimeter. Even if he had managed to do that, how could he, mortally wounded and moving through a mine field, once again climb over the system of fences protecting the Cuban approaches so as to die in his sentry box? The shot that caused his death entered his body at an upward slant. The Cuban sentry box is higher than the place from which the U.S. Marine fired. Moreover, he was shot in the back, yet the U.S. authorities claim he was advancing toward the Marines and was ordered to halt by someone who was ahead of him and who then shot him from the front.

Luis Ramírez López, a 20-year-old farmer, had volunteered for the Revolutionary Armed Forces; he was chosen as a member of the Border Patrol because of his loyalty to the revolution, his proven bravery and his calm approach to daily life. He had planned to become an engineer.

December 7 is the day on which Cubans honor the men and women who gave their lives in the struggles for Cuba's independence. On that day in 1989, while the bodies of Cubans killed while on missions of solidarity in Angola and other parts of the world were being buried, another act of provocation took place. "The guard was changed at 10:02," Lieutenant Luis

Rodríguez Fabier, of the Border Patrol, wrote in the log. At that moment, as he stood in the sentry box of post 17 of the eastern Cuban sector, a bullet fired from just inside the perimeter of the U.S. base missed his forehead by only a few milimeters.

Two hours later, something similar occurred at post 18 in the same sector, very near the place Luis Ramírez López had been murdered. José Angel Castillo, who was standing guard at the time, told the Cuban and foreign press that he was walking along the balcony of the sentry box, observing his designated area, when he suddenly heard the glass in the front window of the sentry box shatter a few centimeters behind him, at a head level. When he turned around, he saw a bullet hole. Ballistics experts who were consulted said that the two bullets came from a special rifle used by a sharp-shooter who fired against both Cuban sentry boxes from near post 13 on the U.S. side. Ten minutes after the second shot, a white pickup truck, presumably belonging to the intelligence service on the base, picked up an individual carrying a rifle who was around 1,500 meters away from the second Cuban post that had been hit.

There is only one obvious guilty party: the U.S. government. There is only one motive: its limitless hostility to the Cuban revolution. Thus, the Guantánamo Base continues to be a powder keg.

Chapter 4

Gunboats again

Current U.S. policy on Cuba seems to reflect the boom in remakes of old U.S. movies. Far from changing with the times and expressing its proverbial pragmatism, the United States' policy of force against its closest neighbor in the Antilles seems to take us back to the days of silent films and the Big Stick, reinstating gunboats — now in the form of aircraft carriers and missile-carrying cruisers — as floating embassies. The Guantánamo Naval Base has become the stage for this second-rate drama successfully fulfilling the mission of maintaining and increasing tension between the two nations.

It could well be said that there is an escalation along the border which implies even greater danger, since it involves complex acts of provocation on a larger scale which have been meticulously planned and have clear consequences. The most recent events in that U.S. military enclave bear this out.

Wolf in sheep's clothing

After the September 1991 coup that deposed the constitutional President of Haiti, Jean Bertrand Aristide, battle troops and matériel were increased at the base under the pretext of evacuating U.S. citizens from that country. In November of that year, a White House spokesman described the sending of more Marines to put up around 10,000 tents for Haitian refugees and maintain order in the enclave. In fact, this "humanitarian" act was used to cover up something entirely different.

In a short period of time, over 300 transport planes of

different kinds landed at the Guantánamo Naval Base, bringing in the men of Joint Task Force 20. They were to take part in Operation Safe Harbor, to be held with the participation of Army, Marine and Air Force units, plus elite and special units, such as the 10th Mountain Light Infantry Division and the 10th Artillery Regiment of the Marines' 2nd Division.

The U.S. government sent in the strongest vigilance and protection body ever seen at the base: a police contingent complete with artillery. Did it mobilize such a contingent during the 1992 riots in Los Angeles? Was it preparing to intervene militarily in Haiti, or to stage a large-scale act of provocation against Cuba that would lead to an invasion? A few days later, the forces that had just arrived at the base began a military exercise that lasted for several days and clearly demonstrated one of the U.S. authorities' real intentions.

The exercise simulated the massive entry of Cuban civilians opposed to the revolution at different points along the border, including a dry run of the evacuation of nonmilitary U.S. personnel and foreigners living on the base. The irresponsible, criminal nature of the exercise was exposed when the radio station in the enclave — which can be heard nearby — stated that the evacuation exercise would include many Cubans. This gave the green light to those Cubans wishing to leave illegally, for it implied that those listening to the call should engage in the extremely dangerous action of challenging the strong system of security established in both directions — which, as has already been explained, includes one of the densest mine fields in the world.

The exercise showed that the U.S. government contemplated this variant in its anti-Cuban plans under the heading "humanitarian intervention," as a response to a hypothetical civil war in Cuba. The White House, which is so ready to talk about human rights — although always with their own interpretation — thus endangered the lives of thousands of Cuban citizens to suit U.S. political interests.

Such an action could serve as a catalyst for another, large-scale action that, in its various phases, could provide grist for the mill of a campaign on supposed human rights violations in Cuba and could lead to a direct aggressive response by the United States.

Prior to the maneuver and as an indispensable complement to it, diverse media in the United States — especially in Florida — "revealed" false accounts of measures the Cuban government was supposed to have taken for deactivating the mine fields and taking down the fences just outside the base so as to permit the massive exodus of those Cubans who hadn't obtained visas for going to the United States — visas denied by the same government that, from its radio station inside the base, was instigating illegal departures. Among other lies, the mass media spread stories of a supposed attack by a Cuban Navy patrol launch against a U.S. fishing vessel and supported the idea of a probable attack by the Cuban Air Force against the Turkey Point nuclear power plant in Florida.

As if this weren't enough, other serious incidents were noted during the exercise, including artillery target practice carried out around 400 meters from the boundary fence with Cuban territory, in the northeast gate sector, instead of at the artillery proving ground inside the base. On that occasion, over 500 shots were recorded, with some of the shells landing near the boundary of the U.S. military installation, which could have had serious consequences. This was one of the most dangerous acts of provocation in recent times.

In other incidents, TA-4J planes permanently based at Guantánamo and a CH-53E helicopter from the reinforcement units have violated Cuban airspace — the planes on five occasions and the helicopter, once. The aircraft were carrying their normal weapons when they overflew the Cuban troops' positions, and the helicopter also carried personnel who had engaged in landing exercises inside the base. CH-53E helicopters and C-130 transport planes have also practiced air landing techniques both by day and night.

The United States' naval presence in the bay has been increased; at moments of maximum tension, over 20 warships, including five missile-carrying cruisers, a submarine and the helicopter carrier *Guam*, have been anchored there. Moreover, NATO ships have entered the bay to offload supplies. In the same period, a naval group composed of six amphibious craft headed by an LPH-12 helicopter carrier with the capacity to disembark a reinforced battalion of Marines was also in the area.

Voices and drums of war

A high-ranking Marine officer explained the exercises on the base by saying that troop training should be carried out in conditions closely resembling those of the place of possible combat, so what could be better than Guantánamo, right on the spot? Well-informed sources say that this has become standard operating procedure of the U.S. Army in recent times, and maneuvers are carried out in tropical areas very similar to Cuba.

In the exercises, the "adversaries" are units that have studied what weapons and possibilities the Cuban units have and assume their structure and composition. For example, units of the 101st Airborne Division, part of the rapid deployment forces, engaged in such actions in the practice maneuvers carried out at the Fort Chaffee, Arkansas, battle training center in September and October 1991. The same thing has happened, using different U.S. units, at other training centers, such as the one at Fort Irwin, where an "adversary" group called the Atlantics assumes the properties of Cuban troops. Moreover, the commentary accompanying these actions, as provided by General Colin Powell, then chairman of the Joint Chiefs of the Staff, the most outspoken of Cuba's opponents, is on a par with the rest of the campaign.

In an interview published in the April 15, 1991, issue of *Navy Times*, General Powell said, "I'm running out of demons. I'm running out of villains. I'm down to Castro and Kim Il Sung." He was even more explicit on arriving at the Guantánamo Naval Base — he was the highest ranking military officer to visit it since the 1962 October Missile Crisis — on January 6, 1992.

On that occasion, he said that danger still existed in the world, which is why the United States had 1,700 young men and women in places such as Guantánamo, because they had a mission to fulfill there. That Vietnam veteran's words represent more than an isolated, hasty comment triggered by circumstance and typify a mentality shaped by other war frustrations; they form a doctrinaire concept that is prevalent at the highest levels of the U.S. military hierarchy.

The Joint Chiefs of Staff's decision to open a special office for monitoring the Cuban situation — an office headed by Frank Libutti, coordinator of the Cuba group, who was General Powell's immediate subordinate — is more proof of that line of thinking. In addition, high-ranking U.S. military officers have appeared before the Armed Services Committees of the Senate and House to set forth their ideas on a probable social outburst in Cuba and a massive, disorderly emigration of Cubans to the U.S. base which could endanger "the national security of the United States." General James Claper, chief of military intelligence, told the members of the Senate Armed Services Committee on January 22, 1992, that the Cuban situation had reached such a point that it could cause problems for the national security of the United States. He said he based his analysis on the rapid deterioration of the Cuban regime's economy, which could quickly lead to generalized violence and a massive, disorderly exodus to the United States by sea or to the Guantánamo installation, among other possibilities.

Admiral Leon A. Edney, chief of the Atlantic Command, told the members of the same committee on March 4, 1992, that Cuba posed the greatest threat to the security of the United States in the Atlantic, for the same reasons given by General Claper. He emphasized that his command was keeping very close tabs on the situation and was preparing to meet any eventuality.

A few weeks earlier, the February 18 issue of the *International Herald Tribune* contained a summary of a 70-page report drawn up by a group of Pentagon experts headed by an admiral who was also deputy chairman of the Joint Chiefs of Staff; it described the theaters of operations for armed conflicts that the United States would probably wage in the coming period. One of those seven places was the Caribbean — including, of course, Cuba.

This line of thinking in top U.S. military circles was given more publicity when an article on the Pentagon's draft strategic plan — directed by then Under-Secretary of Defense Paul D. Wolfowitz — appeared in *The New York Times* on March 8, 1992. It described the supposed internal crisis in Cuba, saying that it implied new challenges for the United States and that, therefore, it was necessary to have a contingency plan for handling everything from a massive exodus of Cubans to the United States, to a military provocation by Cuba against the United States or any of its allies, to a war on the island.

One may well ask why the Supreme Command of the Armed Forces of the United States has suddenly become so interested in Guantánamo — a thing that hadn't ever happened before in the long history of that enclave. High-ranking U.S. military brass have visited Guantánamo more than 40 times, but the two visits that General Colin Powell made to the base in the first three months of 1992 and the five by Admiral Edney, chief of the Atlantic Command, to cite two examples, were particularly notable. Moreover, the head of the United States Interests Section in Cuba visited Guantánamo, too.

Maneuvers or threats?

One of the most recent expressions of the U.S. authorities' hostility toward Cuba was the Ocean Venture '92 exercise, held in areas very close to the island, including the Guantánamo Naval Base, with participation by over 30,000 members of the U.S. elite forces, and dozens of warships and planes. Such exercises are carried out on a regular basis, but this latest one was more threatening than the others because of the U.S. government's intensification of its aggressive policy against Cuba.

The composition of the participating forces, their goal and the main center of action clearly showed against whom the staff of the 18th Airborne Army Corps, the members of the 82nd and 101st Airborne Divisions, the 24th Armored Division, the 10th Mountain Light Infantry Division, the 2nd Marine Expeditionary Force and the Special Operations Forces — all with special previous training on the scene of a probable military intervention against Cuba — were directing their preparations.

Together with those units, more than 20 warships of different kinds from the Atlantic Fleet, including the commands of two aircraft carrier battle groups and aircraft of the 12th Air Force, also participated in the exercise. U.S. military spokesmen had already told the press that the public objectives of the maneuver were to train and check the capacities of a joint force protecting the national interests of the United States and of military support for its allies in the area of responsibility of the Atlantic Command.

U.S. taxpayers should ask themselves why, when all are feeling pinched by the economic recession and their own government says the Cold War and the East-West conflict are over, they should pay for those exercises. Moreover, elementary logic shows that a small, poor country such as Cuba cannot pose the slightest threat to the most powerful nation in the world.

All this shows the furious hostility against Cuba that has prevailed in U.S. policy, bent on stepping up the tension that has existed for so long between the two countries. During the Reagan and Bush years, an imperial atmosphere reigned in the White House, with mistaken, dangerous boasting to the effect that the only enemy left for the United States was "red Cuba."

Chapter 5

Bedrock arrogance

Crushing the Cuban revolution has been a frustrated presidential obsession ever since the Eisenhower administration, for Republicans and Democrats alike. In eight consecutive administrations, this policy has been a stubbornly recurring theme, sustained by force and an ideology of sorts. It is also obvious that the United States' belligerent policy against Cuba in no way reflects a coherent approach to its international relations.

President Bush, for example, defended relations with the People's Republic of China — a nation his administration has accused of having committed serious human rights violations — pointing out that it is better to maintain relations with a transgressing nation in order to influence it and bring it into line. In his time, Ronald Reagan did the same concerning South Africa with his "constructive compromise."

It is said in the United States that the Cold War ended with the collapse of the European socialism and the disintegration of the Soviet Union. How, then, can the U.S. government explain its obsessive interest in destroying the Cuban revolution?

These days the White House has no basis for its main arguments against Cuba, such as the "Soviet threat" from Cuba or the revolution's willingness to support the national liberation movements in Latin America or elsewhere. In 1987 and 1988, the Cuban government freed most of the prisoners who were serving sentences for having committed crimes against the government; in that same period, it allowed human rights groups to visit jails and talk with prisoners.

By virtue of the sovereign decision of Cuba and Angola, the Cuban troops were withdrawn from Angola. Yet in May 1989, shortly after the signing of those agreements, then U.S. Secretary of State James Baker made public a memorandum in which he declared that an easing of Cuba-U.S. relations wasn't possible because, for years, Cuba's conduct hadn't changed in any way to justify such a position.

The White House has been reacting like an ostrich, sticking its head in the sand and refusing to face reality. Moreover, when all other arguments were exhausted, it has resorted to its old arsenal and stepped up its activities in Guantánamo to provoke a conflict that could unleash larger, devastating actions; it has also increased its military presence in the area with exercises such as Ocean Venture. High-ranking government officials, however, have declared that the United States has no intention of attacking Cuba. Under-Secretary of State Robert Gelbard, for example, reiterated the Bush administration position when addressing the Foreign Affairs Committee of the House of Representatives in late 1991.

That statement — pro-peace on the face of it — was aimed at calming sectors of world public opinion that no longer accept the argument that Cuba is a Soviet military springboard for attacking the United States. It was also directed at the U.S. people, since more and more of them fail to view their tiny neighbor as a terrifying version of the Evil Empire, as Reagan described the Soviet Union. And many even want the relations between the two countries to be normalized — as shown in the latest polls on the topic.

Once again, the United States' words are one thing, and its deeds, another, for the evidence of hostility continues. For example, 523 military reconnaissance flights were carried out against Cuba between January 1, 1989, and December 31, 1991. In that same period, U.S. tactical planes based in Florida made more than 80,000 flights to within 100 kilometers of western Cuba, where Havana is located — that is, seven or eight minutes' flying time away for a combat plane.

Most recently, the U.S. Air Force has also intensified its exercises in areas near the island, with strong naval groups, including the battle groups of the aircraft carriers CV-66 *America* and CV-65 *Saratoga*. In addition to these military contingents, ships, planes, radar and other types of sensing devices in the region (supposedly there to combat drug trafficking) engage in constant reconnaissance. An average of 10 to 15 ships and 20 to 25 planes take part in those activities every day.

Cuba is in a difficult situation, for it has lost the support of its allies, the former Soviet Union and other formerly socialist countries. The U.S. response — not only opportunistic but criminal — is to tighten the blockade in an attempt to strangle the Cuban revolution. Its refusal to allow ships from third countries that have touched Cuban ports to enter U.S. ports is an example of this. The Torricelli Bill, which banned trade with Cuba by U.S. subsidiaries in other nations — an act that undermines those nations' sovereignty and also constituted a restriction on free trade — was narrowly adopted by the U.S. Congress in 1992.

The United States' policy of unrelenting hostility to Cuba has failed to bear fruit after more than three decades, even though it has created many problems for Cuba. Therefore, it would be only logical to take a realistic or pragmatic line; in fact, however, the U.S. authorities seem bent on demonstrating the truth of the old refrain that common sense is the least common of our senses.

The United States isn't going to give up its dreams of destroying the Cuban revolution, but it can choose between two paths: that of hostility and aggression and that of peace — with which it could try to influence political affairs on the island through other means. The first alternative has proved to be totally ineffective, although the United States hasn't yet resorted to military intervention, which would inevitably lead to another Vietnam.

It hasn't tried the second alternative. As a matter of principle, Cuba isn't opposed to a policy of peaceful coexistence, and President Fidel Castro has stated that, if the U.S. authorities lift the economic blockade and stop their threats, campaigns and war against Cuba, another form of political leadership in the country could be considered, both in theory and in practice.

Cuba has shown that it can stand firm and knows that its goals are realistic. It is struggling to create an equitable society that meets its needs, without clinging to old, foreign models.

— Because its revolution is of, by and for its people, Cuba is free of the serious ills that led to the demise of European socialism.

When the United States examines its differencies with Cuba, it should dig down to the core, to the essence of the problem. It has tried to show that communism is to blame, but this is not the case. The United States has been set on annexing Cuba come hell or high water since long before the doctrine of communism was formulated, long before the Bolshevik revolution of 1917, long before Fidel Castro led the popular victory over the U.S.-backed Batista dictatorship. Rather, what lies at the heart of this dispute is the U.S. authorities' resistance to seeing Cuba become a free and sovereign nation.

— The Guantánamo Naval Base is the concentrated expression of those unsatisfied geopolitical ambitions and the arrogance of the powerful when faced with something that didn't turn out the way they wanted.

Calm, realistic reflection is worth much more than positions of irrationality and force. Those who govern the United States perhaps should go back — with the humility and greatness of the founding fathers of their nation — to the origins of their homeland and, out of love and respect for their history and for the U.S. citizens they represent, apply the principle of the natural right of every people to determine its own destiny for itself.

Appendix 1

The Breckenridge Memorandum

On December 24, 1897, J.C. Breckenridge, U.S. Undersecretary of War, sent a list of written instructions to Lieutenant General Nelson A. Miles, Commander of the U.S. Army, concerning U.S. aspirations and policy towards the Hawaiian islands, Puerto Rico and Cuba.

A few weeks after the Breckenridge Memorandum was issued, on February 15, 1898, at 10:00 a.m., the battleship Maine exploded in Havana Bay. Two hundred and sixty sailors, the majority of them black, died in that explosion, while the officers, all white, were safe on shore. This incident was used by the United States as a pretext to intervene in the Spanish-Cuban war on the eve of Cuba's victory over Spain.

Department of War
Office of the Undersecretary
Washington D.C.
December 24, 1897

Dear Sir,

This department, in accordance with the departments of foreign trade and the Navy, feels obligated to complete the instructions on the military organization of the upcoming campaign in the Antilles with certain observations on the political mission that will fall to you as general in charge of our troops. Until now, the

43

annexation of territories to our Republic has been that of vast, sparsely populated regions, and such annexation has always been preceded by our immigrants' peaceful settlement, so the absorption of the existing population has been simple and swift.

In relation to the Hawaiian Islands, the problem is more complex and dangerous, given the diversity of races and the fact that the Japanese interests there are on the same footing as ours. But taking into account their meager population, our flow of immigrants will render those problems illusory.

The Antillean problem has two aspects: one related to the island of Cuba and the other to Puerto Rico; as well, our aspirations and policies differ in each case.

Puerto Rico is a very fertile island, strategically located to the extreme east of the Antilles, and within reach for the nation that possesses it to rule over the most important communications route in the Gulf of Mexico, the day (which will not tarry, thanks to us) the opening is made in the Isthmus of Darien. This acquisition which we must make and preserve will be easy for us, because in my mind they have more to gain than to lose by changing their sovereignty since the interests there are more cosmopolitan than peninsular.

Conquest will only require relatively mild measures. Our occupation of the territory must be carried out with extreme care and respect for all the laws between civilized and Christian nations, only resorting in extreme cases to bombing certain of their strongholds.

In order to avoid conflict, the landing troops will take advantage of uninhabited points on the southern coast. Peace-loving inhabitants will be rigorously respected, as will their properties.

I particularly recommend that you try to gain the sympathy of the colored race with the double objective of first obtaining its support for the annexation plebiscite, and second, furthering the main motive and goal of U.S. expansion in the Antilles, which is to efficiently and rapidly solve our internal race conflict, a conflict which is escalating daily due to the growth of the black population. Given the well-known advantages that exist for them in the western islands, there is no doubt that once these fall into our hands they will be flooded by an overflow of black emigrants.

The island of Cuba, a larger territory, has a greater population density than Puerto Rico, although it is unevenly distributed. This population is made up of whites, blacks, Asians and people who are a mixture of these races. The inhabitants are generally indolent and apathetic. As for their learning, they range from the most refined to the most vulgar and abject. Its people are indifferent to religion, and the majority are therefore immoral and simultaneously they have strong passions and are very sensual. Since they only possess a vague notion of what is right and wrong, the people tend to seek pleasure not through work, but through violence. As a logical consequence of this lack of morality, there is a great disregard for life.

It is obvious that the immediate annexation of these disturbing elements into our own federation in such large numbers would be sheer madness, so before we do that we must clean up the country, even if this means using the methods Divine Providence used on the cities of Sodom and Gomorrah.

We must destroy everything within our cannons' range of fire. We must impose a harsh blockade so that hunger and its constant companion, disease, undermine the peaceful population and decimate the Cuban army. The allied army must be constantly engaged in reconnaissance and vanguard actions so that the Cuban army is irreparably caught between two fronts and is forced to undertake dangerous and desperate measures.

The most convenient base of operations will be Santiago de Cuba and Oriente province, from which it will be possible to verify the slow invasion from Camagüey, occupying as quickly as possible the ports necessary for the refuge of our squadrons in cyclone season. Simultaneously, or rather once these plans are fully in effect, a large army will be sent to Pinar del Río province with the aim of completing the naval blockade of Havana by surrounding it on land; but its real mission will be to prevent the enemy from consolidating its occupation of the interior, dispersing operative columns against the invading army from the east. Given the impregnable character of Havana, it is pointless to expose ourselves to painful losses in attacking it.

The troops in the west will use the same methods as those in the east.

Once the Spanish regular troops are dominated and have withdrawn, there will be a phase of indeterminate duration, of partial pacification in which we will continue to occupy the country militarily, using our bayonets to assist the independent government that it constitutes, albeit informally, while it remains a minority in the country. Fear, on one hand, and its own interests on the other, will oblige the minority to become stronger and balance their forces, making a minority of autonomists and Spaniards who remain in the country.

When this moment arrives, we must create conflicts for the independent government. That government will be faced with these difficulties, in addition to the lack of means to meet our demands and the commitments made to us, war expenses and the need to organize a new country. These difficulties must coincide with the unrest and violence among the aforementioned elements, to whom we must give our backing.

To sum up, our policy must always be to support the weaker against the stronger, until we have obtained the extermination of them both, in order to annex the Pearl of the Antilles.

The probable date of our campaign will be next October [1898], but we should tie up the slightest detail in order to be ready, in case we find ourselves in the need to precipitate events in order to cancel the development of the autonomist movement that could annihilate the separatist movement. Although the greater part of these instructions are based on the different meetings we have held, we would welcome from you any observations that experience and appropriate action might advise as a correction, always, in the meantime, following the agreed upon lines.

Sincerely yours,

J.C. Breckenridge

[Retranslated from a Spanish version of the Memorandum]

Appendix 2

The Platt Amendment

That in fulfillment of the declaration contained in the joint resolution approved April twentieth, eighteen hundred and ninety-eight, entitled "For the recognition of the independence of the people of Cuba, demanding that the Government of Spain relinquish its authority and government in the island of Cuba, and to withdraw its land and naval reserve forces from Cuba and Cuban waters, and directing the President of the United States to carry these resolutions into effect," the President is hereby authorized to "leave the government and control of the island of Cuba to its people," so soon as a government shall have been established in said island under a constitution which, either as a part thereof or in an ordinance appended thereto, shall define the future relations of the United States with Cuba, substantially as follows:

I. That the government of Cuba shall never enter into any treaty or other compact with any foreign power or powers which will impair or tend to impair the independence of Cuba, or in any manner authorize or permit any foreign power or powers to obtain by colonization or, for military or naval purposes or otherwise, lodgement in or control over any portion of said island.

II. That said government shall not assume or contract any public debt, to pay the interest upon which, and to make reasonable sinking fund provision for the ultimate discharge of which, ordinary revenues of the island, after defraying the current expenses of government shall be inadequate.

III. That the government of Cuba consents that the United States may exercise the right to intervene for the preservation of Cuban independence, the maintenance of a government adequate for the protection of life, property, and individual liberty, and for discharging the obligations with respect to Cuba imposed by the Treaty of Paris on the United States, now to be assumed and undertaken by the government of Cuba.

IV. That all Acts of the United States in Cuba during its military occupancy thereof are ratified and validated, and all lawful rights acquired thereunder shall be maintained and protected.

V. That the government of Cuba will execute and as far as necessary extend, the plans already devised or other plans to be mutually agreed upon, for the sanitation of the cities of the island, to the end that a recurrence of epidemic and infectious diseases may be prevented, thereby assuring protection to the people and commerce of Cuba, as well as to the commerce of the southern ports of the United States and of the people residing therein.

VI. That the Isle of Pines shall be omitted from the proposed constitutional boundaries of Cuba, the title thereto being left to future adjustment by treaty.

VII. That to enable the United States to maintain the independence of Cuba, and to protect the people thereof, as well as for its own defense, the government of Cuba will sell or lease to the United States land necessary for coaling or naval stations at certain specified points, to be agreed upon with the President of the United States.

VIII. That by way of further assurance the government of Cuba will embody the foregoing provisions in a permanent treaty with the United States.

From U.S. Statutes at Large, *XXI, 897-898; Treaty between the United States and Cuba, signed in Havana May 22, 1903; proclaimed by President Theodore Roosevelt July 2, 1904.*

Bibliography

Archives of the Revolutionary Armed Forces. Border Patrol. Museum of History.

Benítez, José A.: "200 años de codicia, hostilidad y agresiones" (200 years of greed, hostility and aggression), *Granma*, Havana, May 28, 1980.

D'Estéfano Pisani, Miguel A.: *Cuba, Estados Unidos y el Derecho Internacional Contemporáneo* (Cuba, the United States and contemporary international law). Ed. Ciencias Sociales, Havana, 1983.

Film and video archives of the Revolutionary Armed Forces Movie and Television Studios (ECITVFAR).

Foner, Philip S.: *Historia de Cuba y sus relaciones con Estados Unidos* (History of Cuba and its relations with the United States). Ed. Ciencias Sociales, Havana, 1973.

Gómez, Máximo: "En una guerra un hombre es un número, la idea lo es todo" (In a war, a man is a cipher, the idea is everything), *La Nación Cubana*, no.9, year 3, 1986, Havana, Cuba.

"Que prepara Estados Unidos en Guantánamo" (What the United States is preparing in Guantánamo), editorial in *Granma*, May 5, 1992.

Toste Ballart, Gilberto: *Guantánamo: USA al desnudo* (Guantánamo: The USA laid bare). Ed. Política, Havana, 1990.

Yglesia Martínez, Teresita: *Cuba, primera república, segunda ocupación* (Cuba: First republic, second occupation). Ed. Ciencias Sociales, Havana, 1976.

Main acts of provocation and violations at the Guantánamo Naval Base

No.	1962	1963	1964	1965	1966	1967	1968	1969	1970	1971	1972	1973	1974	1975	1976	1977	1978	1979	1980	1981	1982	1983	1984	1985	1986	1987	1988	1989	1990	1991
1	8	2																										1		1
2	309	71	88	169	79	2					2	1	2	2	1				4		1	6	2	7	10	1		1		1
3	3	34												2																2
4	222	98	155	87	10	9			1		4	9			2	1		2	2	3	28	3	4	4			4	1		2
5		1																												
6	13							6					2	2																
7	21	365	101	26	20	5	10		6					2	2				1			3	38	1	1		1	3		
8	4	2	2	2							1	2		3	5				1	3	1	6	8	1	1					
9	236	439	612	40	4						2		1	5				2	7	2	3	8			1	2	1	2	3	5
10	17	3	3	3								1	1													2				
11	25	12	2																											
12	488	363	316	121	17	17	3		1		4	1	4	14	3	2		1	3	16	4	48	3	10	4			2	3	3
13	106	1	85	145	22	22	7				1			75						4	21	21		17	10				1	33
14	10																													
15		3																												
16		1																												
17	953	75	15	62	26	52	2	21	25	8	26	13	6	3	3	3		2	3		7	21	10	4	1	1		1	2	12
18	4912	524	112	58	15	56	47	107	62	51	45	26	8	17	7	3		43	109		1	24			5			5	9	12
19		1					1		1									1	6	5										
20																		6												
TOT.	7317	1989	1496	713	193	185	88	138	94	60	79	46	21	132	15	19	5	130	67	10	38	165	65	43	35	6	7	12	16	56

1. Throwing objects from planes.
2. Shooting with rifles and pistols toward non-occupied territory.
3. Shooting with pellet guns toward non-occupied territory.
4. Aiming with rifles toward non-occupied territory.
5. Aiming with machine guns toward non-occupied territory.
6. Aiming with cannon and tanks toward non-occupied territory.
7. Crossing the border by land.
8. Showing lack of respect for the Cuban flag.
9. Throwing stones and other objects toward non-occupied territory.
10. Engaging in pornographic and other obscene acts.
11. Provoking incidents toward non-occupied territory.
12. Making comments, gestures, etc. that are offensive to Cuban sentries.
13. Using lanterns and reflectors to illuminate non-occupied territory.
14. Breaking boundary fences.
15. Directing fire hoses against non-occupied territory.
16. Making landings with military helicopters in non-occupied territory.
17. Violating Cuba's jurisdictional waters with military launches and ships.
18. Violating Cuba's jurisdictional waters with military helicopters and planes.
19. Climbing the boundary fence.
20. Engaging in other acts of provocation and violations.

Index

Also published by Ocean Press

Changing the history of Africa: Angola and Namibia
Edited by David Deutschmann
Why did more than 300,000 Cubans — of all ages and professions, men and women, black and white — volunteer to help defend Angola from repeated South African invasions? Was the presence of these Cuban forces in Angola an obstacle to Namibia's independence and peace in the region? Were they a threat to U.S. security as Washington often claimed? With contributions from Colombian writer Gabriel García Márquez, as well as Fidel Castro, Jorge Risquet, and Raúl Castro, this book helps to provide a background to the events in Southern Africa.
175 pages plus 32 pages photos, ISBN paper 1-875284-00-1

A new society — Reflections for today's world
By Ernesto Che Guevara
Has socialism a future? Che Guevara's perspective on the transition to a new society in the early years of the Cuban revolution as presented in this selection contributes to the discussion in the world today on the future of socialism. This book is the product of Che Guevara's experience as the President of the National Bank, the Minister of Industry, and as a central figure in the revolutionary government.
234 pages plus 16 pages photos, ISBN paper 1-875284-06-0

Cuban women confront the future
by Vilma Espín
How has family life in Cuba changed since the revolution? How are Cuban women confronting the discrimination and prejudices of the past? How do they see their gains and the challenges still facing them today? Vilma Espín is the president of the Federation of Cuban Women.
95 pages, ISBN paper 1-875284-23-0

Can Cuba Survive?
An interview with Fidel Castro
In a frank exchange with Mexican journalist Beatriz Pagés, Cuban leader Fidel Castro confronts the realities of Cuba in a "new world order." In this book length interview he considers the issues facing his own country. What is the situation in Cuba since the collapse of the socialist countries of Europe? Are socialism and democracy compatible? What chance is there of Latin American integration? How should Latin America respond to the 500th anniversary of Spanish colonization? What real power does Fidel Castro have in Cuba? Why is Cuba an obsession for the United States? How does Fidel Castro see his personal role in Cuba and his place in history? Lastly, Cuban President Fidel Castro accepts the challenge to answer the most controversial question: Can Cuba survive?
105 pages, ISBN paper 1-875284-58-3

Tomorrow is too late — Development and the environmental crisis in the Third World
by Fidel Castro
During the most controversial and widely discussed speech to the 1992 World Earth Summit in Rio, Cuban President Fidel Castro caught the imagination of the summit's delegates when he cast blame for the world's environmental crisis on Western consumer societies and called for the use of science to sustain development without pollution. Comprising Castro's speech and the text of the document prepared for the delegates, this book presents the international environmental crisis in a new and important perspective.
54 pages, ISBN paper 1-875284-73-7

Island in the storm
The Cuban Communist Party's Fourth Congress
Edited by Gail Reed
Island in the storm describes Cuba's strategy for survival, as it emerged from the most critical meeting in the revolution's history.
200 pages, ISBN 1-875284-48-6

The Cuban Revolution and the United States
A Chronological History
by Jane Franklin

An invaluable resource for scholars, teachers, journalists, legislators, and anyone interested in international relations, this volume offers an unprecedented vision of Cuban-US relations. Cuba watchers will wonder how they got along without it. Based on exceptionally wide research, this history provides a day by day, year by year report of developments involving Cuba and the United States from January 1, 1959, through 1990. An introductory section, starting with the arrival of Christopher Columbus in the Caribbean, chronicles the events that led to the triumph of the revolution in Cuba in 1959. Indispensable as a reference guide, *The Cuban Revolution and the United States* is also an eye-opening narrative, interrelating major crises with seeemingly minor or secret episodes. Published in association with the Center for Cuban Studies.

276 pages, ISBN paper 1-875284-26-5

Cruel and unusual punishment
The U.S. blockade of Cuba
by Mary Murray

Is Washington's trade ban with Cuba an embargo, as the U.S. government claims, or an illegal blockade? *Cruel and unusual punishment* will help you make up your mind. Does the policy violate international law, the United Nations' Charter and the principles of the Organization of American States? Is it, as Cuba says, one of the worst human rights violations ever committed by one country against another? *Cruel and unusual punishment* details the blockade from its inception in 1960 until today. Mary Murray walks you through Cuba's perspective on the blockade, using the knowledge she gained while working on the island as a journalist. This book presents Cuba's argument as heard by the General Assembly of the United Nations and offers the latest evidence of the U.S. campaign to win outside support for its Cold War against Cuba.

117 pages, ISBN paper 1-875284-78-8

Fidel and Malcolm X — Memories of a meeting

by Rosemari Mealy

The first extensive account of the 1960 encounter between Fidel Castro and Malcolm X in Harlem's Hotel Theresa. With testimonies from contemporaries of both figures, the story is told of the stay in Harlem of Castro and the Cuban delegation after they were forced from a downtown Manhattan hotel. Previously unpublished photos are included, along with Amiri Baraka's (LeRoi Jones) award-winning 1959 essay "Cuba Libre."

80 pages plus 16 pages photos, ISBN paper 1-875284-67-2

Face to face with Fidel Castro

A conversation with Tomás Borge

The issues confronting a changing world are frankly discussed in this lively dialogue between two of Latin America's most controversial political figures. In this wide-ranging conversation, Fidel Castro discusses the collapse of the Soviet Union, an historical evaluation of Stalin, the future of socialism, the role of ideas in today's world, Cuba's relations with the United States from Kennedy to Bush, human rights in the Third World, homosexuality, literature and music. One of the most important political books to emerge from Latin America in the 1990s.

181 pages, ISBN 1-875284-72-9

Che — A memoir by Fidel Castro

Edited by David Deutschmann

For the first time, Fidel Castro writes with candor and affection of his relationship with Ernesto Che Guevara, documenting the Argentinian-born doctor's extraordinary bond with Cuba from the revolution's early days to Che's final guerrilla expeditions to Africa and Bolivia. Included are Castro's descriptions of Che's personal traits, his last days with Che in Cuba, and a remarkably frank assessment of the Bolivian mission. Illuminated by many newly published photos — including the first and last of Guevara and Castro together — this is a revealing portrait not just of its subject but of its author as well.

165 pages plus 24 pages photos, ISBN paper 1-875284-15-X